HOUGHTON MIFFLIN

Reading

A Legacy of Literacy

Here We Go!

Senior Authors
J. David Cooper
John J. Pikulski

Authors
Patricia A. Ackerman
Kathryn H. Au
David J. Chard
Gilbert G. Garcia
Claude N. Goldenberg
Marjorie Y. Lipson
Susan E. Page
Shane Templeton
Sheila W. Valencia
MaryEllen Vogt

Consultants
Linda H. Butler
Linnea C. Ehri
Carla B. Ford

 HOUGHTON MIFFLIN   BOSTON • MORRIS PLAINS, NJ

California • Colorado • Georgia • Illinois • New Jersey • Texas

Cover and page photography by Michelle Joyce.

Cover illustration by Nadine Bernard Westcott.

Acknowledgments begin on page 256.

Printed in the U.S.A.

ISBN: 0-618-01226-5

23456789-DW-06 05 04 03 02 01 00

All Together Now   12

realistic
fiction

Big Book: Ten Dogs in the Window
by Claire Masurel
illustrated by Pamela Paparone
🏅 Bank Street College Best Children's
Books of the Year

Phonics Library:
Nan Cat
Fat Cat
Tan Fan

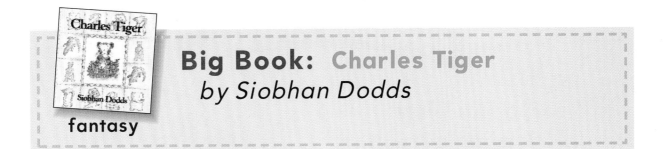

On My Way Practice Readers

Cat
by Alice Lisson

Fan Cat Can Jump
by Iris Littleman

One Big Hit
by Kathryn Lewis

Theme Paperbacks

Bear Play
by Miela Ford

Dan and Dan
*by Marcia Leonard
photographs by
Dorothy Handelman*

I Had a Hippopotamus
by Hector Viveros Lee

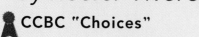 CCBC "Choices"

Contents
Theme 2

Surprise! 128

Dot Fox
by Denise Zimmer
illustrated by Dominic Catalano

Dot Fox got a wig.

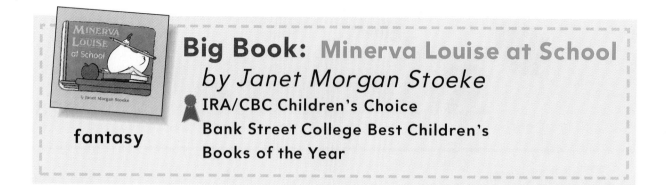

Big Book: Jasper's Beanstalk
*by Nick Butterworth and
Mick Inkpen*
Best Books for Children
United Kingdom Children's Book Award

fantasy

Phonics Library:
The Bug Kit
Quit It, Zig!
Rug Tug

On My Way Practice Readers

Five Big Boxes
by Irma Singer

The Pet
by Maria Cara

Where Is Tug Bug?
by Oscar Gake

Theme Paperbacks

**"What Is That?"
Said the Cat**
*by Grace Maccarone
illustrated by Jeffrey Scherer*

The Pet Vet
*by Marcia Leonard
photographs by
Dorothy Handelman*

Spots
*by Marcia Leonard
photographs by
Dorothy Handelman*

To read about more good books, go to Education Place.

www.eduplace.com/kids

This Internet reading incentive program provides thousands of titles for children to read.

www.bookadventure.org

All Together Now

Read Together

Because we do
All things together
All things improve,
Even weather.

**from the poem
"Together"
by Paul Engle**

Words to Know

go   cat

the   sat

The cat sat.

Go, cat.

Meet the Author and Illustrator
Lynn Munsinger

The Cat Sat

written and illustrated
by Lynn Munsinger

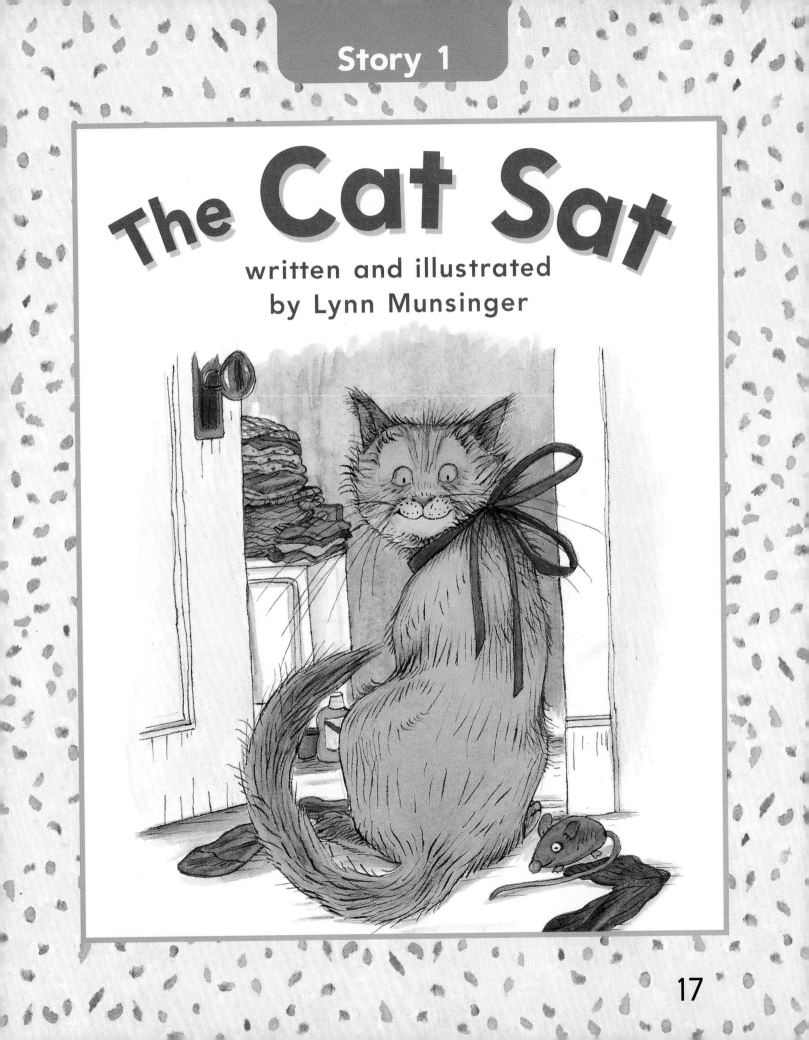

The cat sat.

Go, cat!

The cat sat.

Go, cat!

The cat sat.

Go, cat!

The cat sat.

Think About the Story

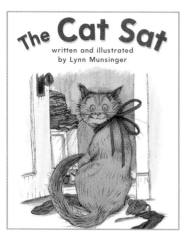
The Cat Sat
written and illustrated
by Lynn Munsinger

 Why did the girl say "Go, cat"?

 What was the best place for the cat to sit?

3 How would you get the cat to move?

26

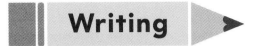
Write a Label

Draw and label a picture of the cat. Share your picture.

The Mat

Words to Know

on	cat
the	sat
go	mat

Cat sat.

Cat sat on the mat.

Go, Cat!

Meet the
Author and Illustrator
Nadine Bernard Westcott

The Mat

by Nadine Bernard Westcott

Cat sat on the mat.

Cat, Cat, Cat! Go, Cat.

Cow sat.

Goat sat.

Dog sat.

Cat sat.

Go!

41

The mat sat on Cat.

Think About the Story

The Mat

by Nadine Bernard Westcott

1 Why do you think the animals sat on the mat?

2 Why did the woman yell "Go"?

3 Would you want animals in your house? Why?

Writing

Write a Sign

Make a sign to help keep
the animals out of the house.

Cats

Cats are furry, cats are small
Cats are hardly big at all
Cats can purr and cats can mew
Do you like cats?
I sure do!

by Jacquiline Kirk, Age 9
Mauritius, Indian Ocean

At Night

When night is dark
my cat is wise
to light the lanterns
in his eyes.

by Aileen Fisher

Nan and Fan

illustrated by Lisa Campbell Ernst

Words to Know

not	Fan
jump	can
here	tan
and	pat
Nan	fat

Nan can jump.
Fan can not.

Nan and Fan can go here.

Nan can pat the fat tan cat.

Meet the Illustrator
Lisa Campbell Ernst

illustrated by Lisa Campbell Ernst

Nan can go.

Fan can not.

Nan can jump.

Fan can not.

Nan can pat the fat tan cat.

Fan can not.

Nan can go here.

Fan can not.

Go, Fan!

Nan can go.

Fan can go.

Think About the Story

illustrated by Lisa Campbell Ernst

1 Why did Fan follow Nan?

2 Why can't Fan go to Nan's school?

3 What would you do if a pet followed you to school?

Write a List

Make a class list of pets. Write "Our Pets" at the top of the list.

We Can!

written by Diane Hoyt-Goldsmith
photographs by Joel Benjamin

Words to Know

here	fan
we	An
and	Nat
too	Pat
can	

An can fan.

An and Pat can fan.

Nat can fan here, too.
We can fan!

Meet the Author

Diane Hoyt-Goldsmith

Meet the Photographer

Joel Benjamin

We Can!

written by Diane Hoyt-Goldsmith
photographs by Joel Benjamin

Here we go!

An can go.

Pat can go, too.

An can read.

Pat can, too.

An can write.

Nat can, too.

An can draw.

Pat can, too.

Nat can, too.

An, Nat, and Pat can fan!

Think About the Story

written by Diane Hoyt-Goldsmith
photographs by Joel Benjamin

1 What can the children do at school?

2 Do you think the children like school? Why?

3 Would you like to go to their school? Why?

Describe a Character

Use punch-out letters to make a character's name. Then write one word to describe the character.

The More We Get Together

The more we get together,
    together, together,
The more we get together,
    the happier we'll be.
'Cause your friends are my friends,
    and my friends are your friends,
The more we get together,
    the happier we'll be.

Traditional

The Big Hit

The **Big Hit**

written by
Angela Shelf Medearis

illustrated by
John Ceballos

Words to Know

who	big
find	hit
a	bat
have	ran
one	

Who can find a big, big bat?

We have a big bat.

Nan can hit one.

Nan ran.

Meet the Author
Angela Shelf Medearis

Meet the Illustrator
John Ceballos

The Big Hit

written by
Angela Shelf Medearis

illustrated by
John Ceballos

Who can find a big bat?

We have a big bat.

Who can hit?

93

94

Nat can hit.

Go, Nat, go!

Nat ran, ran, ran.

Nan can hit.

Nan ran, ran, ran.

Pat hit a big one.

We ran, ran, ran!

Responding

Think About the Story

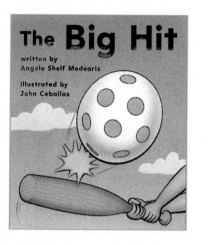

The Big Hit
written by
Angela Shelf Medearis

illustrated by
John Ceballos

1 Do you think the children like to play ball? Why?

2 Why did the children chase the dog?

3 How would you get the ball from the dog?

104

Writing

Write a Name

Draw your favorite character from the story. Write the character's name.

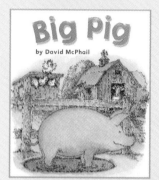

Words to Know

a	big
find	pig
have	fig
one	fit
who	sit
to	hat
	ran

Who can Big Pig find?
Go to Nan, Big Pig.

Big Pig ran.

Sit, Big Pig.
Have one big fat fig.

Can a hat fit Big Pig?

Meet the Author and Illustrator
David McPhail

Big Pig

by David McPhail

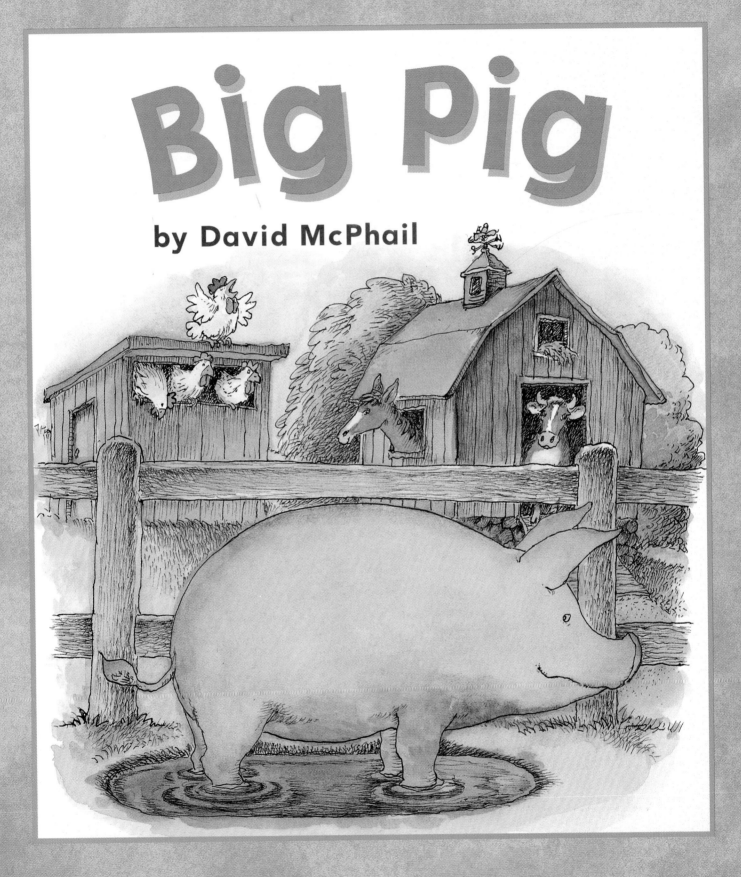

Chapter 1

We go to the farm.

We find a big hat at the farm.

Can the hat fit Matt?

Can the hat fit Nan?

Who can have the big hat?

Big Pig can have the big hat.

Chapter 2

Feed Big Pig.
Sit on Big Pig.

Who can sit on Big Pig?

Big Pig can have one fat fig.

Nan can sit.

Big Pig can have one carrot.

Matt can sit.

Go, Big Pig, go!

Big Pig ran!

Think About the Story

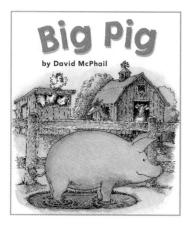

1 Why does Big Pig get the hat?

2 Why did Nan and Matt sit on Big Pig?

3 Would you like to visit Big Pig's farm? Why?

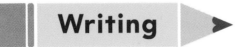 **Writing**

Write a Menu

What does Big Pig like to eat?
Draw a picture and label it.

There Was a Small

There was a small pig who wept tears
When his mother said,
   "I'll wash your ears."
As she poured on the soap,
He cried, "Oh, how I hope
This won't happen again for ten years!"

by Arnold Lobel

126

Pig Who Wept Tears

Surprise!

Read Together

No matter where
  I travel,
No matter where
  I roam,
No matter where
  I find myself,
I always am
  at home.

**from the poem "Riddle"
by Mary Ann Hoberman**

The Box

The Box

written by Andrew Clements
illustrated by Cynthia Jabar

Words to Know

in	Dot
once	got
what	lot
Dan	box
wig	fox

Once Dan and Dot got a big box. What can fit in the big box?

A wig can fit.
A fox can fit.

A lot can fit in the big box.

Meet the Author
Andrew Clements

Meet the Illustrator
Cynthia Jabar

132

The Box

written by Andrew Clements

illustrated by Cynthia Jabar

Once Dan got a box.

What can fit in the box?

A tan fox can fit.

A pig in a wig can fit.

A big hat can fit.

A lot can fit in the box.

Dot got the box.

What can Dot find in the box?

Dot can find a tan fox.

Dot can find a pig in a wig.

Dot can find a big hat.

A lot can fit in a box.

Think About the Story

1 How many things did Dan put in the box?

2 What might Dot do with the things in the box?

3 What would you put in the box?

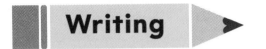

Write a Description

Draw something you would put in the box. Write about your picture.

Wigs in a Box

Words to Know

upon	wig
in	Dan
what	Dot
two	lot
three	box
four	Fox
five	Ox

What can we find in the big box upon the big tan mat?

 Fox got wig one.

 Ox got wig two.

 Cat got wig three.

 Dot got wig four.

 Dan got wig five.

 What a lot in a big box!

Meet the Author and Illustrator
Valeria Petrone

Wigs in a Box

by Valeria Petrone

Who can win the big box
upon the shelf?

153

Pat Pig can hit the ball in.

What can Pat Pig find
in the big box?

Pat Pig can find a wig.

Pat Pig can find one, two,
three, four, five wigs!

Wig one can fit Pat Pig.

Wig two can fit Dot Fox.

Wig three can fit Dan Dog.

Wig four can fit Fat Cat.

Wig five can fit Tan Ox.

Thanks a lot, Pat Pig!

Think About the Story

1. What plan did Pat Pig make when he saw the wigs in the box?

2. Why did the animals thank Pat Pig?

3. Which wig would you choose?

Write a Character Description

Use punch-out letters to write your favorite character's name. Then write some words to tell about the character.

Here Is

Here is the beehive.
Where are the bees?

Hidden away where
nobody sees.

Watch and you'll
see them come
out of the hive.

the Beehive

One, two, three, four, five.

Bzzzzzzzz... all fly away!

167

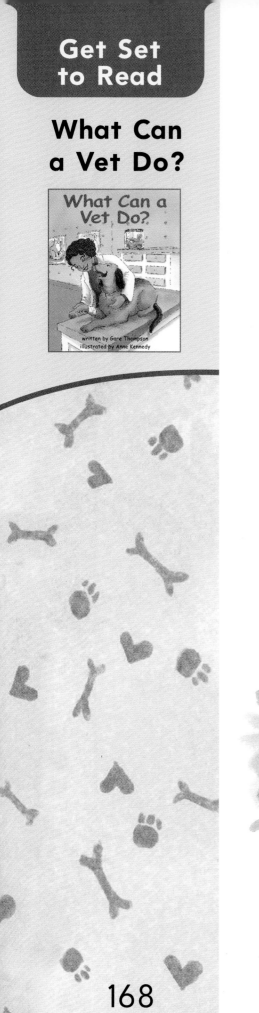

Words to Know

my	yet
do	pet
for	get
is	wet
kit	Ben
vet	pen

Ben is my pet.
Do not get wet, Ben.

Is Ben at the vet?
Not yet.

Get in the pen, Ben.
The vet can get a kit.
What can the vet do for Ben?

Meet the Author
Gare Thompson

Meet the Illustrator
Anne Kennedy

170

What Can a Vet Do?

written by Gare Thompson
illustrated by Anne Kennedy

Chapter 1

What bit my pet cat Big Ben?

Get my pet cat to the vet!

What can the vet do?
The vet can get a kit.

Big Ben can sit.

Big Ben can get wet.

The vet can pat Big Ben.

The vet can do a lot for Big Ben!

Chapter 2

My big pet is in the pen.

Get the vet!

Is the vet here yet?

Here is the vet in a tan van.

What can the vet do?
The vet can get a big kit.

The vet can do a lot!

Think About the Story

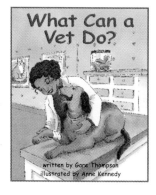

What Can a Vet Do?

written by Gare Thompson
illustrated by Anne Kennedy

 1 What does a vet do?

 2 How do you know the girl and the boy care about their pets?

 3 Would you like to be a vet? Why?

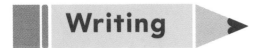
Write a Description

Draw a picture of a pet at the vet.
Write about your picture.

Hot Fox Soup

Words to Know

do	kit
said	vat
my	yet
me	met
is	get
you	wet
I	hen

Hen got a big kit.
Hen got a big vat.
Hen met Fox.

"What can I do?" said Fox.
"I can get you wet," said Hen.
"Here is my vat. Get in."
"Not me," said Fox.

"Get wet," said Hen.
"Not yet," said Fox.

Meet the Author
and Illustrator
Satoshi Kitamura

HOT FOX SOUP

by
SATOSHI KITAMURA

Fox wanted hot hen soup.

Fox got a big, big vat.
Fox lit a hot, hot fire.

Fox got a noodle soup kit.

Fox met Hen.

"What can I do?" said Hen.

"Get wet in my vat," said Fox.

"Not me," said Hen.

Fox met Pig.

Fox wanted hot pig soup.

"What can I do?" said Pig.

"Get wet in my vat," said Fox.

"Not me," said Pig.

Fox met Ox.

Fox wanted hot ox soup.

"What can I do?" said Ox.

"Get wet in my vat," said Fox.

"Not me," said Ox.
"I can not fit."

"You can fit," said Ox.
"We can get hot fox soup!"

"Not hot fox soup!" said Fox.
"We can get hot, hot noodle soup."

207

"Is it hot yet?" said Ox.

"It is hot, hot, hot," said Fox.
"Dig in!"

Think About the Story

1. Why wouldn't the animals get in Fox's vat?

2. How did Ox surprise Fox?

3. Would you eat soup with Fox? Why?

Writing ➤

Write a Sign

Make a sign with the words
Hot_____Soup. Add your own
word to complete the sign.

Polly, Put

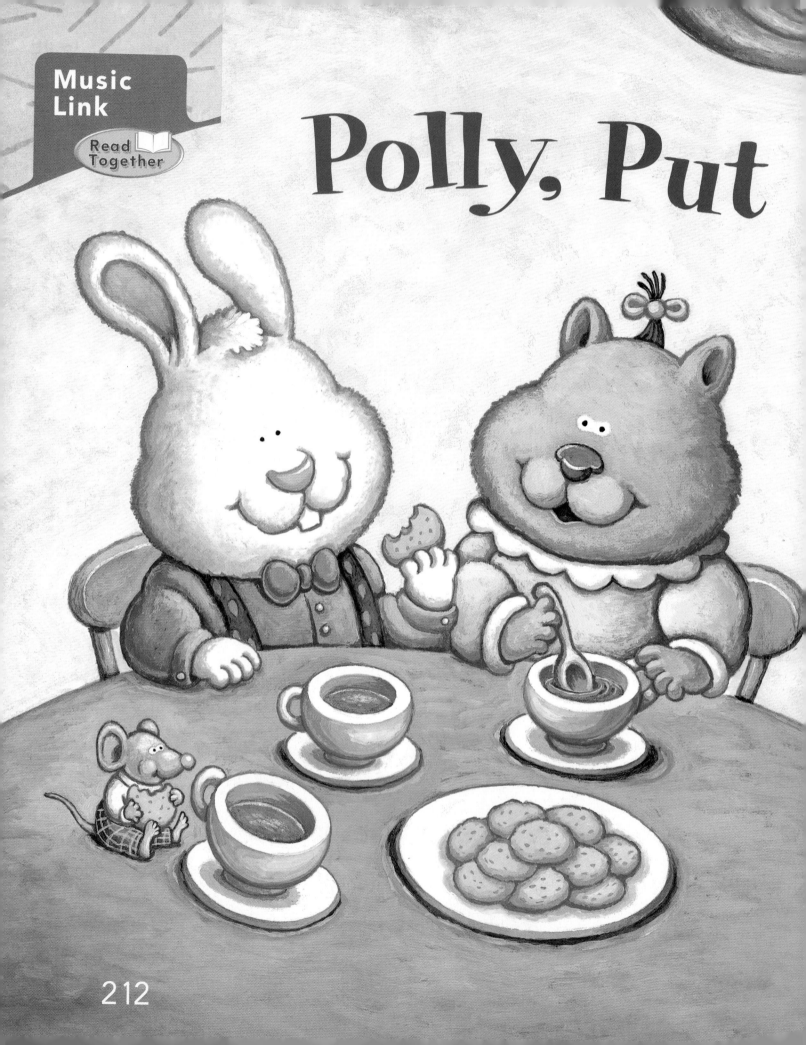

the Kettle On

Polly, put the kettle on,
Polly, put the kettle on,
Polly, put the kettle on,
We'll all have tea.

English Traditional Song

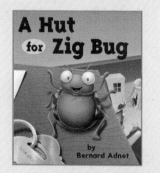

Words to Know

does	hut
he	jug
live	Bug
where	rug
quit	tug
Zig	

Where does Zig Bug live?
Does he live in a hut?

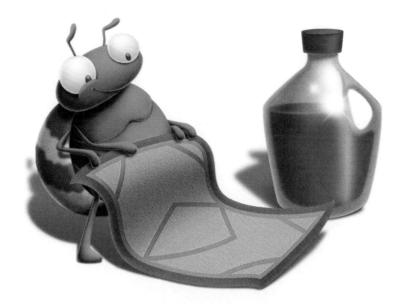

Zig Bug can get a jug.
Zig Bug can get a rug.

Do not quit, Zig Bug!
Tug, tug, tug!

Meet the Author and Illustrator
Bernard Adnet

A Hut for Zig Bug

by
Bernard Adnet

Does Zig Bug have a hut?
He does not.

Where can Zig Bug live?
Can Zig Bug live here?

Can Zig Bug live in a box?

Can Zig Bug get a cot in the hut?

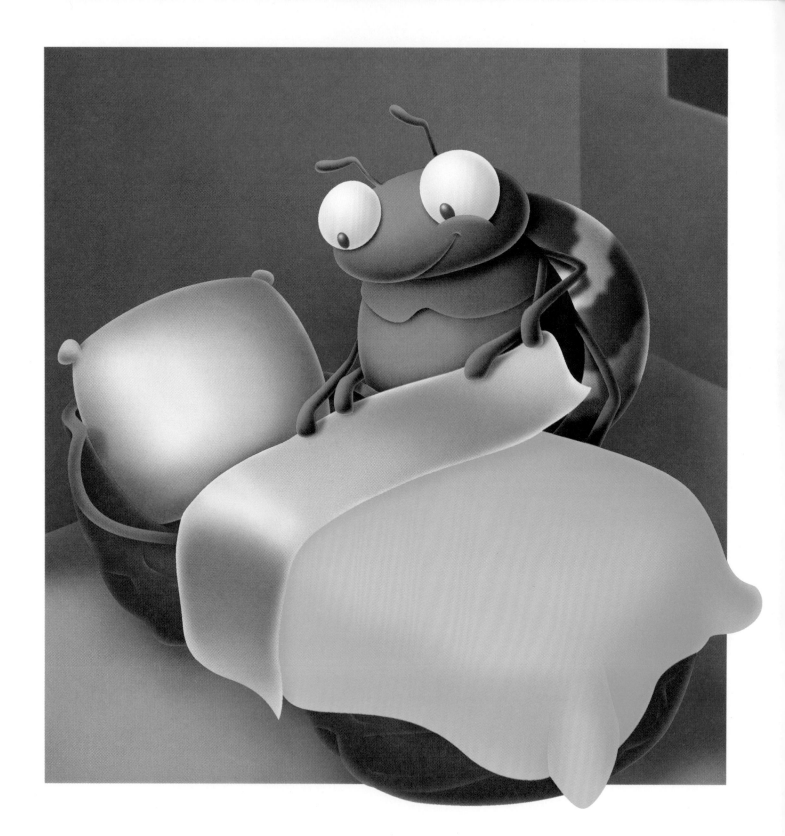

The cot can fit in the hut.

Can Zig Bug get a jug in the hut?

The jug can fit in the hut.

Can Zig Bug get a rug in the hut?

The rug can fit in the hut.

Can Zig Bug get a pan in the hut?

The pan can fit in the hut.

Can Zig Bug fit in the hut?

Do not quit, Zig Bug!

Zig Bug can live in the hut!

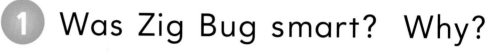
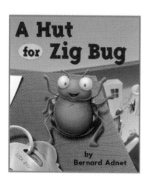

A Hut for Zig Bug
by Bernard Adnet

Think About the Story

1 Was Zig Bug smart? Why?

2 What else could Zig Bug put in his hut?

3 Will Zig Bug be happy in his hut? Why?

USA 33
Bombardier beetle

Write a List

List the things Zig Bug put in his hut. Add some more things he could put in there.

The Rope Tug

Words to Know

are	zig
does	jig
pull	hut
they	but
away	tug
quit	

Cat is in a big hut.
Can Rat pull Cat away?

"You are big," said Rat.
"But I can tug."
They tug, tug, tug.
Zig, zig, zig!

"I quit," said Cat.
The rat does a jig.

Meet the Author
Veronica Freeman Ellis

Meet the Artist
Mary Lynn Carson

Meet the Photographer
Richard Haynes

236

The Rope Tug

written by Veronica Freeman Ellis • art by Mary Lynn Carson

photography by Richard Haynes

Narrator

Elephant

Hippo

Rat

Elephant can get in the hut.
Hippo can get in the hut.

But Rat can not get in.
Rat can not fit.

Let me in.

 You can not fit, Rat.
Go away, Rat!

 I can pull you outside.
I'm not big, but I can tug.

 You can not tug me.

 You can not tug me.

 Can you pull me?
I'm not big, but I can tug.

We are big!
We can pull you!
Get a big rope, Rat!

 Rat can get a big rope.

 **Rat can zig, zig, zig.**

Tug, tug, tug!

They are big!
They can tug, tug, tug.
But they can not pull Rat.

I quit!

I quit!

 Rat does a jig.

I'm not big, but I can tug.

Read Together

Think About the Story

1 Why wouldn't Elephant and Hippo let Rat in the hut?

2 How did Rat surprise Elephant and Hippo?

3 How else could Rat have gotten Elephant and Hippo out of the hut?

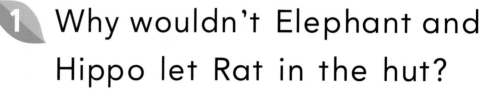

Write a Description

Draw your favorite part of the play.
Write some words to tell about it.

Way Down South

Way down South where
bananas grow,
A grasshopper stepped on
an elephant's toe.
The elephant said, with tears
in his eyes,
"Pick on somebody your
own size."

Anonymous

Acknowledgments

For each of the selections listed below, grateful acknowledgment is made for permission to excerpt and/or reprint original or copyrighted material, as follows:

Poetry

"At Night" from *Out in the Dark and Daylight,* by Aileen Fisher. Copyright © 1980 by Aileen Fisher. Used by permission of Marian Reiner for the author.

"Cats" by Jacqueline Kirk. Copyright © by Jacqueline Kirk. Reprinted by permission of the author.

"Here Is the Beehive" from *Hand Rhymes,* collected and illustrated by Marc Brown. Copyright © 1985 by Marc Brown. Published by Dutton Children's Books, a division of Penguin Putnam Inc.

"Riddle" from *The Llama Who Had No Pajama: 100 Favorite Poems,* by Mary Ann Hoberman. Copyright © 1973 by Mary Ann Hoberman. Reprinted by permission of Harcourt Inc.

"There was a small pig who wept tears. . ." from *The Book of Pigericks: Pig Limericks,* by Arnold Lobel. Copyright © 1983 by Arnold Lobel. Reprinted by permission of HarperCollins Publishers.

"Together" from *Embrace: Selected Love Poems,* by Paul Engle. Copyright © 1969 by Paul Engle. Reprinted by permission of Random House, Inc.

Credits

Photography

3 (t) image Copyright © 2000 PhotoDisc, Inc. **7** (t) image Copyright © 2000 PhotoDisc, Inc. **12** (icon) image Copyright © 2000 PhotoDisc, Inc. **12–13** Jo Browne/Mick Samee/Tony Stone Images. **16** Courtesy Lynn Munsinger. **27** (cat) Artville. **30** Courtesy NB Westcott. **44** Artville. **46–7** Artville. **50** Courtesy Lisa Campbell Ernst. **64** (l) American Images Inc./FPG International. (r) Jeri Gleiter/FPG International. **68** (t) Lawrence Migdale. (b) Mark Gardner. **82** images Copyright © 2000 PhotoDisc, Inc. **84–5** Telegraph Colour Library/FPG International. **88** Andrew Yates/Mercury Pictures. **89** Dennis Gray/Mercury Pictures. **104** images Copyright © 2000 PhotoDisc, Inc. **108** Sharron McElmeel. **124** images Copyright © 2000 PhotoDisc, Inc. **125** (r) image Copyright © 2000 PhotoDisc, Inc. **128** (icon) image Copyright © 2000 PhotoDisc, Inc. **128–9** Mauritius/Nawrocki Stock Photo Inc. **132** (t) Jon Crispin/Mercury Pictures. (b) Courtesy Cynthia Jabar. **150** Courtesy Valeria Petrone. **170** (t) Kindra Clineff. (b) Courtesy Anne Kennedy. **186** image Copyright © 2000 PhotoDisc, Inc. **190** Courtesy Farrar, Straus and Giroux. **210** image Copyright © 2000 PhotoDisc, Inc. **216** Courtesy Bernard Adnet. **236** (t) Jesse Nemerofksy/Mercury Pictures.

Assignment Photography

66–67, 69–81 Joel Benjamin; **26–7, 45, 65, 83, 105, 125** (l), **146–7, 164–5, 166–7, 187, 211, 232-3, 253** David Bradley Photographer; **236** (m&b) **234–5, 237–252** Richard Haynes.

Illustration

14–25 Lynn Munsinger. **28–43** Nadine Wescott. **48–63** Lisa Campbell Ernst. **86–103** John Ceballos. **106–123** David McPhail. **70–81(t)** Rob Dunlavey. **126–127** Stef De Reuver. **130–145** Cynthia Jabar. **148–163** Valerie Petrone. **166–167** Tammy Smith. **168–185** Anne Kennedy. **188–209** Satoshi Kitamura. **212–213** Matt Novak. **214–231** Bernard Adnet. **234–251** Mary Lynn Carson. **254–255** Keiko Motoyama.